CW0677133

E Collar Training 2021:

Everything You Need to Know to Effectively Train Your Dog with an E Collar

Jenna Jimenez

Table of Contents

Chapter 11: Other Problems the E Collar Can Help You Solve with

Introduction

Congratulations on purchasing *E Collar Training*, and thank you for doing so.

The following chapters will discuss all of the things that you need to know when it comes to e collar training. There is a lot of controversy when it comes to this kind of training. Some dog owners are big proponents of this training method, saying it was the most effective and fast method for them to train their dog to behave, even when they are not there. And on the other side of things, plenty of dog owners feel that this training method falls flat and that it is not the best for any dog owner to work with.

While it is true that the e collar should not be the only training method that you use with your dog, and in fact, it should be used in conjunction with some other training methods as well, there is no denying the progress that can come when you want to fight off some disruptive behaviors with your dog quickly. This guidebook is going to go over the basics of e collar training, how to pick out a good collar, how to be safe with this collar, and even some of the steps that you can use to teach your dog how to behave with this collar.

The first part of this guidebook is going to explore all of the things that you need to know when it comes to the e collar. We will look at some of the basics of the e collar and how to use it safely, some of the benefits and potential drawbacks that come with this kind of collar, and even the accessories that are needed to make sure that it works right. We will also explore a bit about how to properly fit the collar on the dog, and how to make sure you get the right stimulation for your dog to ensure they feel and respond to it, without causing the dog any harm or pain along the way.

Next, we will take a look at some of the different training techniques that you are able to use with this collar. We will explore the steps that you need to use when it comes to off-leash training and perimeter training, and even some of the basics about using commands with the training or when you should just rely on the collar for the best results.

The end of this guidebook will help us to learn a bit more about the basics of e collar training. We will talk about some of the forms of correction that you can use with this collar, how to handle some of the different distractions that your dog may face, and then answer some of the most common questions that dog owners have when it comes to using and seeing results with this kind of collar on their dog.

Training your dog is a process that takes some time and some patience along the way. Whether you are just trying to get a good head start with your training or you have a bad behavior that has appeared in your dog, and you want to get it taken care of sooner rather than later, the e collar may be the right choice to add into your training methods. When you are ready to learn a bit more about e collar training and some of the benefits, as well as the steps that you need to know to get started, make sure to check out this guidebook today!

There are plenty of books on this subject on the market, thanks again for choosing this one! Every effort was made to ensure it is full of as much useful information as possible. Please enjoy!

Chapter 1: The Tools That You Need for E Collar Training

When it comes to training your puppy, there are a lot of different options that you can choose from. Often working with treats, praise, and other rewards will be the trick that your puppy needs to learn. Others want to find methods that are a bit faster because they are short on time or won't be able to stay home and deal with properly training their puppy. And others may need to deal with some problem areas with their dog, and they need to find something new that will help them out.

There are a ton of tools that you can use, and you can consider which method is going to work the best for you. But here, we are going to explore the idea of the e collar and why it may be the choice that you need to help with training your puppy and getting them to behave in the manner that you would like.

What is the E Collar?

Before we start to look at some of the particulars that come with the e collar, we first need to explore what this device really is. An e collar is going to be an electronic collar or a shock collar, that can help you to properly train your puppy to act in the manner that you would like. There are some pet owners who are not fond of these because they feel that it is not effective, that they are providing a shortcut that doesn't help with the bond between a dog and their owner, and they worry that these collars are going to be painful for the puppy.

Despite some of these claims, you will find that the e collar is not going to be painful, and it can be a really good method of training your puppy to act in the manner that you want. There are actually a lot of benefits and arguments that go for the use of the e collar, and maybe some of them are the reason why you decided to work with the e collar in the first place. Some of the arguments for using these e collars with training your puppy will include:

1. They are not going to be any different than other forms of training. There are some dog trainers who will use the e collar and who claim that when used properly, the stimulus from the collar is going to be no different than a little tug on the leash or something similar that you may use with your puppy.

2. The technology that goes with these e collars has improved over the years. When these were first invented, it was impossible to adjust the shock level. The ones that are made today can be adjusted based on the type of dog you have and how much you want to use it. The lowest level of these is so low that even a small dog won't be able to fil it. You can adjust the level so that it annoys your dog, but it won't cause harm.

3. For some types of dogs, these collars are going to be the most effective way to train them. Trainers who decide to use these collars are going to claim that certain types of dogs are going to respond better to a stimulus from the collar than from other types of reinforcement.

Before you jump on board and decide to use the e collar for your needs, there are a few things that you should consider. Always remember that while this can be a good training tool in some cases, you have to use it responsibly, and you have to remember that it is not going to work for all dogs. Taking care to determine if it is working for your dog and if it is the right option for you is going to make a big difference.

The first thing to consider when you want to work with this kind of collar is to remember it should not be the only training tool that you use. There is a ton of evidence out there that points to how positive stimuli for your dog is going to be more effective when you are trying to train them. Rewarding your dog with some treats or another reward when they perform the right behavior, teaching them what the word no means, and using verbal commands work well for most dogs.

If you are using these options in the proper manner, you will probably find that the use of the e collar can be limited for just a few behaviors that the dog does, and you can't seem to break. For example, if you have trouble with them barking all of the time, or they have some leash aggression, you can use the collar to help out with those problems. But for other types of commands and other parts of your training, consider taking the collar off and using other methods.

Another thing to watch out for is whether you have a dog that is aggressive or not. If you find that your dog is more on the aggressive side, the collar is not going to be the best. If you start to train without the collar, and you find that during those sessions, the dog becomes more aggressive when you scold them, then they are not going to respond the best to the shock, no matter how low the level is. Aggressive dogs are not going to do well with this kind of collar, and you will need to pick another training method.

Once you have determined that the shock collar is going to be the best option for you, check out a few options, and determine which collar is going to be the best for your needs. There are three different types of these e collars that you are able to choose from, including obedience collars, bark collars, and containment systems. Each of these is going to be a bit different, so you will need to choose the one that will work the best for your training needs.

First, let's take a look at the containment system and the barking collars. These are going to provide the stimulus automatically to the dog when they do whatever behavior they are not supposed to do. Obedience collars are a bit different in that they have a remote so that the trainer is able to be in control over the stimulus and can decide when to use it and when not to.

Your goal with using this kind of collar is going to be to find a comfortable shock setting that works the best for your dog. The key here is to find the level of stimulus that is going to be high enough that it gets your dog to pay attention but still low enough that it won't end up causing the dog any pain. A good indicator of this is going to be when you press the button for the collar. You should see the dog perk up their ears and turn their head like they are saying, "What was that?"

If you are using the collar and they yelp or put their tail between their legs, this is a sign that the shock is too strong for the dog. A good way to make sure that you can get the right stimulus level for your dog is to pick out one collar that is going to have a high number of stimulation levels so that you can choose the best level that will be effective without hurting the dog. You can also choose to hold the collar to your hand to test the different levels of vibration to see what is best for them.

You can also pick out a collar that is going to beep. Most of the e collars that you are able to pick out will also have the option of delivering a beep along with the shock. If the dog starts to associate the beef with that negative stimulus, you may find that the beeping will be enough to control the behavior you want without even needing to use a shock. You will need to use the shock to start with, but over time, you can switch over to just using the beeps instead.

As you are using the collar with the remote, try to hide the remote as much as possible. If your dog starts to see the remote and they associate it with the shock, they are going to start having a fear of the remote control, and in some cases, they are going to be more aggressive to it. They will associate the remote as the bad thing, rather than seeing that their negative behavior is the reason they are getting that stimulus.

As with any kind of training method that you try to use with your dog, you need to be the responsible one. If you use this electronic training, the most important thing to remember is to use the collar in a responsible manner. Watch the training videos that come with the particular collar that you decide to work with so that you are sure that you are really using it in the proper manner.

The goal of the e collar is to teach the dog how you would like them to behave. You want to give them a little bit of shock that is annoying but not one that is going to harm them. You want it to be a way to get them to pay attention and start changing up the behaviors that they use, but not something that they use all of the time. In fact, it may be something that you only use outside, for example, to make sure the puppy listens to you or doesn't bark to other people and animals all of the time, and then the rest of the day, the collar is taken off.

If you are worried about using it in the wrong manner, you plan to leave it on all day, you don't have any other training methods set up to work with the dog on, or you plan to turn up the frequency too high, then this is a sign that the e collar is not the right option for you. There are a lot of other training methods you can use as well, but for some dog owners, this is the best and most effective one, especially when it comes to dealing with some unwanted behavior that the dog is just not willing to give up. When it is used responsibly, it will help your dog to learn the behaviors you want and can make the training process that much easier.

Types of Devices You Can Use

The good news here is that you can pick from a few different devices that you would like to work with. Each of these will work in a different manner based on what your goals are and what the dog needs to work on. Let's take a look at the three most common methods that you are able to use and the three device types that will work the best for most dogs.

First, we have the pet containment system. This is the most common type of the e collar. The point of these containment systems is that it will help to keep your dog inside a space of the home without needing to have a physical barrier. If you want to make sure that while you are gone, the dog stays in one area, then you could set up that parameter so that they don't end up leaving it.

These can even be used outside of the home, such as in the backyard. For some areas where it is hard to make a physical fence, or you don't have the money to put one up, you can use this collar to make sure that the dog will stay in the back and not try to run off from you. You get to choose the area where you would like the puppy to stay while they are wearing the collar.

There are a few different options that you can go with. You can choose a more in-ground installation. Lots of owners who are making an outside fence with the use of the collar will like this method because it will help to keep the lawn looking nice even though there isn't a fence or anything in place. You can do an above-ground installation of the collar to help reinforce a barrier that is already there but still isn't enough to keep the dog contained. And then, if you want to work with this collar to restrict where the dog is able to go into the house, you can use a system that is wireless.

For the most part, the pet containment system is going to work when you are able to install a wire around the perimeter of the yard. This wire is perfectly safe because it is not going to have any current. This is a nice change to another option of the electric fence. These fences are going to carry a current that is at a high voltage that can easily get too strong for your dog. Instead, the wire for the collar is going to form up a closed-loop with a circuit box that can then transmit out a radio signal to the receiver.

This receiver is going to be on the collar that you put on your dog. Then, once you get it all set up, the dog is going to notice and feel that the collar will activate any time they get close to the perimeter that you set. If they stay away from it, then they won't feel anything from the collar at all.

The next type of e collar that your dog can have based on your needs is a bark collar. These are often used by dog owners in order to curb nuisance or excessive barking. When the dog starts to bark, when you have the collar on, they will get a little shock right away. These can be activated with the use of a vibration or a microphone, and some of the collars that you can go with are going to use both the vibration and the sound to help make sure that any noises around the dog are not causing the collar to go off.

And the third option that you can choose when you are picking out an e collar is going to be a training collar or a remote trainer. Training collars of this kind are going to be activated with the help of a device that you can hold onto. Better quality remote trainers are going to have a lot of functions and levels that you can pick with. This helps you to decide how long the stimulation should go on, the quality of the stimulation, and you can even add in some vibration and a beep to the stimulation to make sure you get the attention of the dog ahead of time.

This one is nice because it gives you the full power that you need to take care of your dog properly. You can pick the one that your puppy is most likely to need based on what problem you would like to see fixed. If you have a dog that likes to bark often, then the bark collar would be the best. If you want to use the collar to help with various training techniques and with the training commands, then the training collar is the best. Or, if you just want to make sure that the puppy stays in a specific part of the home or stays in your yard, then the pet containment system is going to be the best for your needs.

Technical Considerations

Understanding how the collar is going to work can make a big difference in the amount of success that you are able to get when you use this collar. It can also help you to understand that your dog is going to be just fine when you use the collar, as long as you decide to use it in a responsible and caring manner. When it is used as a gentle way to train your dog, rather than as a punishment, it is going to be a great tool to include in your arsenal.

The electric shock is going to be characterized on this collar in terms of voltage, current, frequency of the waveform, waveform, pulse rate, and duration. Although the duration of the shock, the current, and the voltage can come together to calculate the amount of energy that is applied, they are not going to be the best indicators of how intense the stimulus is or how the recipient, in this case, the dog, is going to perceive it.

Often, we don't realize how strong something is going to be. A static electric shock, for example, is going to be around 20,000 to 25,000 volts. We have this just by bumping into someone, and it is not going to be painful or damaging to us in any way physically because the current on them is so low. This is the same kind of idea that comes with these collars. The current is going to be so low that your dog is just going to notice it but won't be hurt.

Depending on the way that the collar is designed, the collar may be set in a way so that the shock given to your dog is just a bit uncomfortable and nothing more. Variable settings on the collar will be important so that you can adjust the levels to what the dog needs, and you can change it as they grow up as well and need more.

In some cases, these collars are going to be referred to as delivering more of a static shock. The thing to remember here, though, is that the static electricity is going to be a direct current, and it will carry little energy. These collars are going to work more on alternating current ideas. This is why it is not really accurate to refer to the e collars as delivering just a static shock to the dog.

To make sure that there is consistent stimulation when you want it, you need to make sure that good contact is made between the electrodes on the collar and the skin of your dog. The manufacturer is going to send some instructions on how to fit the collar correctly on your dog to ensure that it fits and that your dog is not getting harmed in the process. Local humidity and the coat density of the dog, the surface conductivity, and the skin thickness will all come into play as well.

To make this work the best, you will need to experiment a bit and see what is going to work with your dog. Always try it on yourself first to make sure that it is not too strong. But you may start out with a low pulse and find that it does not work with your dog and will slowly increase it from there. Then there are some dogs who can take a lower pulse and be just fine as well. It all depends on your dog, how big they are, and how they respond to the stimulus.

Things to Consider When Using the Collar

Before you decide to go with this kind of collar to help you with training, you need to take a few things into consideration. This is not meant to be a training tool that is going to cause pain or be a punishment for the dog. It is not meant for you to just sit back and do none of the training yourself. And it should not be the only training method that you are going to use.

If you plan to cause pain and use the electronic collar as a form of punishment, then it is probably best not to get a dog at all. This is one of the main reasons that many dog owners are against using this kind of collar in the first place. They don't want to find out that a dog is getting harmed in the process because of a negligent owner.

In addition, the collar is used as another source to train the dog, not as a source of punishment. If you are running inside to grab the collar each time the dog decides not to listen to you, then you need to reconsider using it at all. Bringing it into the training sessions is not a bad thing. But it should be part of the training and not used to punish the dog during the learning process.

You should also not use this as a lazy way to train your dog. It is fine if it is used to help you speed up the process, such as being worried about the puppy running out of your yard to a busy street or stopping your puppy from barking when you are already in trouble for it. But you also need to be involved in the training. Working with the dog to show them where their boundaries are, and teaching them some of the basic commands will make a world of difference in how well they listen to and communicate with you, and can make it so that the collar is barely something that you need.

Along the same lines, the e collar should never be the only training method that you decide to use. It may seem like an easy way to do it, but you need to also form a good bond with your dog, and show them the right way to behave, whether they have the collar on or not. An e collar is a great tool, but it should not be on all of the time, and you should not rely on it too much.

A good way to make sure that you don't become too reliant on the collar is to pick out certain times each day when you are allowed to use it, and that is the only time. Maybe you want to make sure the dog stays within a certain enclosure in the backyard, or you want to stop barking. Then the collar would only be on when they are outside, and the rest of the time, you resort to using other training methods instead.

What to Look for in These Collars

The next thing that you may want to consider when you decide the electronic collar is the right choice for you is what you need to look for when you want to pick out the right one. Having a good idea of what you should look for in a shock collar is going to be important in picking out the one that works for you and your dog. Just like with any other product that you look for, there are going to be a high and a low end in the products, and the price is not always going to be the same as quality.

Most of the time, these collars are going to cost a good amount of money, which means that most owners want to make sure that they are picking out a unit that is higher in quality, that works, and that has a lot of options that go with it. For example, there are a lot of units that are low to mid-range that may work well, but then the battery will die out on them after just a few months, and you either have to go without the collar for some time, or you will have to go and spend a lot of money again.

If you don't already know someone who has one of these collars for their dog that you can ask about, then it is time to find some reviews done on the different products and use those to help you out. Sites like Amazon have a long list of training collars that you are able to take a look at. Pay attention to the good and the bad about the product and decide if this is something that you would like to get or not.

There are a few things that you want to look for when picking out a dog shock collar. You want one that is made well and is not going to fall apart when your dog runs and jumps around. You want to find one that is waterproof because you never know when the dog is going to jump into some water or be outside when a sudden downpour happens. And you want to check out the battery and make sure that it is not going to go bad on you too quickly.

Tips on Using These Collars on Your Dog

As a dog owner, you may know that the training process is going to take some time, and it won't always be as easy as you may think in the beginning. And you may know that the e collar is going to be the best option to help you get the training done faster and more efficiently. But you may be at a loss for how you are able to get the collar to work and some of the best practices for using this with your dog. Some of the tips that you are able to use in order to get the most out of training your dog how to behave with these e collars will include some of the following:

1. These training collars are meant to be an aid for training. You should use commands that are consistent before you use the button to send the shock. Teach the dog how to follow the commands and give them time to learn, rather than just getting trigger happy and pushing down on it all of the time.

2. The settings, in the beginning, need to be low. Start out with one of the lowest settings and see whether or not the dog responds. You can then go up slowly until the dog starts to respond a bit.

   a. You don't want them to yelp or cry in pain. But a little notice of the shock, like looking up at you or looking around to figure out what is going on, is just fine. With a bit of experimenting, you will find what will work the best for them and what doesn't hurt them.

3. After your dog has gone through a few of the shocks to get the feeling of them, you can use the vibration in place as a type of warning. This is a good reminder for the dog about what is going to come next if they decide not to listen. Over time, your training may only use the vibration rather than the shock at all.

4. Use the bad beep before you give any of the shocks. This is something that the dog is able to catch on to, and they will soon respond to the sound.

5. Use the good sound, or learn how to praise your dog any time that they respond to the sound in the manner that you would like.

6. If you are training for the dog to stay in your yard, you should consider doing a bit of pre-training before you bring in the shock here.

7. To make sure that the battery lasts as long as possible, you want to do some charging on a frequent basis and do not let the battery stay in the charging position for days at a time, or you will end up ruining the battery in no time.

The Advantages of Using the Shock Collar

There are a lot of people who worry about using this kind of collar on their dog. They feel like it is going to cause a lot of damage to their dog or that it could turn them very aggressive. The truth is, these can potentially happen, but that is if you don't use the collar in the right manner. If you set it up too high, use the collar too much, or don't teach the dog that their behavior is the reason the collar is going off, then it could potentially cause problems.

There are things that you can do to use the collar in a responsible way. For example, trying the collar on your arm or wrist first to see how strong the shock is before putting it on your dog can help you see how strong it is. Your goal with this is not to make the dog get hurt or be in pain in the process. It is all about showing them how to behave, and a little annoyance from the collar can help make this happen.

There are a few advantages that come with using this kind of collar in order to help you train your dog. First, this kind of collar is going to be effective when you are trying to send your dog a signal if you are far away. You can adjust the amount of current that is used, and you can use just a beeping sound to train your dog to behave to that without even needing to shock the dog. You may need to do the shocks in the beginning along with the beeps. Then, over time you can take the shocks away, and the beeping will be enough to get the dog to behave for you.

These collars are a good way to train your dog on how to listen. Some training needs to be done right away, such as when your dog chooses to bark non-stop when they are outside. This can also be effective at keeping your dog safe if they tend to like to run away from you when you go outside, or they like to explore in areas where they should not be. Training them with the collar will ensure that even a difficult dog will start to listen to you, but you must always use this in a responsible manner.

There are some disadvantages to using this kind of collar, though. First, they can be expensive, and you have to decide if this expense is worth it for you or if you would rather use some of the other training methods. If you are not careful with some of the settings that come with this kind of collar, it is possible that they are going to be too harsh. And some dogs respond well to praise and treats and won't really need to have this kind of collar at all. This is why it is so important to learn the temperament of your dog in particular and keep that in mind when deciding if you need one of these or not.

Remember that when you do buy an e collar, you should also get a collar that can be used on a regular occurrence. Your electronic collar is not something that the puppy should wear all of the time. It is a training tool, and this means that the puppy should be allowed to have some breaks from the collar, rather than having to wear it all of the time.

Picking out an e collar and deciding to use it for your needs can be a big decision. It helps you to work on some of the training that is needed with your dog, even though there are a lot of people who feel that this is really not something that is necessary to do with the dog at all. You have to determine your own training needs, and combine it with the way that your dog is responding to other training methods, the safety of your dog (even if it is only the safety in certain areas where you would use the collar) and how fast you need to work on solving the behavioral problem.

By learning how to use the electronic collar in the proper manner, and ensuring that you are going to try it out first, use it along with other training methods rather than all on its own, and paying attention to how much you actually use this collar, you will be able to find one that works for your dog, and soon they will be trained to listen to your commands and do what you would like.

Chapter 2: Things to Know Before Purchasing an E Collar

Before you run out and decide to purchase one of these e collars, it is important to understand how these e collrs work and some of the benefits and negatives that come with using these. You also want to make sure that you understand what to look for when you pick out these collars and some of the benefits that come with it. Some of the things to remember when you decide to go with one of these e collars include:

You Can Adjust the Intensity

One of the neat things that come with these kinds of collars is that you are able to adjust the amount of intensity that comes with them. You can even choose to work with the vibration mode or a warning beep rather than just the shock level. And the level of the shock can be adjusted based on what works for you and for your dog.

For those who are worried about using the shock collar because they think it is going to harm their dog, knowing that you can have a lot of control, and use different modes, can be really comforting and nice. Other collars, including the spray collars that administer a harmless but foul-smelling blast up the nose of your dog, are not going to be adjustable, which gives this kind of collar a leg up on the competition.

Fast results

Many dog owners like to go with this kind of collar because it helps them to get some fast results to help with training. In fact, when it is used in the proper manner, it only takes a few shocks in order to correct most of the unwanted behavior that happens in your dog. And once those few shocks are done, you will be able to use the warning vibration to get the dog to behave in the manner that you want.

This is great news. After a few little shocks that are more uncomfortable rather than anything else, you will be able to rely just on the vibration or the beep that comes with the collar. This helps to keep the dog safe and will make it easier to get the results that you want without having to shock your dog all of the time. Some dogs are a bit more stubborn with this, and you may need to shock them a few more times, but you will be pleasantly surprised at how little you will need to get the dog to listen and how quickly you can stop using the shocks.

You Don't Have to be Nearby All the Time

Shock collars, when you use them properly to control barking that is chronic, can even be used when you are not out with the dog, say when you are gone for work for the day. This can be helpful when you need to leave the dog outside while you are gone, and the neighbors complain about the barking. The same goes for when you use the shock collar to help with controlling boundaries, though you do need to be there in the beginning to do hands-on training with the dog.

Now, there are some people who would not want to leave their dog on the collar unattended because this means that overcorrecting can occur, and you are not there to observe and adjust the situation as needed. But the choice is yours, and most dogs are going to be just fine being on the collar without any help from the owners.

They are Affordable

When you are debating whether to get a shock collar or not as a training device, when you compare it to getting a fence or a professional dog trainer, you will find that the collar is going to be a lot less expensive. Most of the time, these are going to be around $250 for the higher-end models, but you can find them for a bit cheaper.

You will want to determine the features that you are able to find when you work with this kind of product. Some may give you control over the collar with a remote, some allow you to adjust the warning and the shock levels, some will give you a range of distances that the dog can go through, and some even have more than one collar available at a time.

Check through all of the specifications that come with these kinds of collars ahead of time. This will ensure that you are not picking out something that is not going to work or may cause pain to the dog without you knowing what is going on.

The Negatives that Come with the Shock Collars

Before we move on from all of this positive and all of the good things that we are able to get from the shock collars, it is important to see some of the drawbacks and why some people are so against using these collars in the first place. Remember, though, that while these may be valid complaints for some, often a good dog owner, someone who is using it as a tool and will use other positive reinforcement along the way, will not experience any issues with this kind of collar at all.

The first issue that can sneak in is that owners are worried about the shock. Many times, the dog owner doesn't want to cause any pain to their own pet. Keep in mind that these collars are going to allow you to control the amount of intensity that you give to the dog with this shock, but you are still going to give them a little shock that can be uncomfortable for the dog.

Another issue is that the collar could end up causing fear to some dogs. Fear in any animal, especially a dog, is going to be dangerous, so you have to make sure that you are using the collar as a training method that doesn't rely on fear. If the collar is not used in the proper manner, it could cause the dog to learn how to fear situations, objects, and even people that they may associate back with the collar.

You may find that a problem is going to occur with overcorrection sometimes. Without you actually there to watch the e collar, and when you can't watch the shock that is given out, there is a chance that the electric fence and the automatic bark collars are going to deliver shocks too often, or when they are not even needed. This is going to confuse the dog, or it could correct a problem that isn't even there to start with.

And the big reason that a lot of people are worried about working with this kind of collar is that they worry that it doesn't provide the dog with any positive reward, which means that the good behavior of the dog is not being reinforced when you use the collar.

Positive reinforcement is going to include things like a treat, verbal approval and praise, and your attention. So while this kind of collar can be effective at deterring some of the negative behaviors that you want to avoid, like barking all of the time, there is an issue with it not helping you to reward and promote some of the positive behaviors that you want them to keep on doing. This is why with any kind of training program, you want to make sure that there is some positive reinforcement.

This problem is easily fixed if you choose to use the e collar just as a training tool, rather than using it for all of the training. This allows you to still find plenty of other opportunities during the day to reward the positive behavior while using the collar to avoid some of the negative behaviors that you are not fond of the dog using. Putting these all together can make a difference in how well the dog will behave and can ensure that your dog knows how to do what you want, no matter what you are training them on.

There are a lot of good benefits that come with using this kind of collar to help you to train your dog and get them ready to exhibit the behaviors that you want them to. But it is most important for you to be present when the collar is being used. This will ensure that the dog is only getting the shock when they need it and can prevent issues with the dog not getting a positive reward or the shock going off at the wrong times and the dog not learning the behavior that you want them to.

Learning how to use the collar as a way to train your dog and figuring out the schedule that works the best for you both so that the dog can actually learn the behaviors that you want them to is going to be critical here. It will help you to watch that the problems are improving and to be on top of anything that may go wrong with the collar.

Chapter 3: The Accessories You Need

One thing that you need to consider when picking out your e collar is what kind

of accessories you will need. Most reputable companies are going to give you a

battery with the e collar that is long-lasting and that you are able to recharge with

relative ease. If this is not offered with the collar, then you need to make sure that

you are purchasing a battery so that you can actually use the collar the way that

you want. You can also choose from a few different styles of collars that you

would like to work with. And one of the most important things about this is that

you will have some access to a variety of contact points based on the one you

choose to go with.

So, purchasing one of these collars that comes with batteries you can recharge is critical. There are some options that are lower in price, but the battery is not rechargeable, and you will find that you are replacing the batteries more often than you want. And when you have to replace them all the time, there is a bigger pain because they are special ones that aren't easy to find at your local stores. Yes, the units with the rechargeable battery may be more expensive, but in the long run, getting this kind is going to really save you. A good quality collar of this kind will have rechargeable batteries in the collar as well as these in the remote.

Another upgrade that you may want to consider working with is a bungee collar. There is an attachment like this that can work for the majority of e collars and are able to help these stretch out to the size that your dog will need. You will find that all of the e collars are either going to have a collar that is one inch or .75-inch-wide, so it is easy to find these bungee collars for any of the electronic collars you choose to purchase.

This is such a great thing to do. While you will see how to fit the collar on your dog in the next chapter, it is possible that your dog's neck will go up in size a bit when they are running around, and their temperature rises. The bungee collar is a good addition to deal with this so that the collar is not too small when they are running around and not too big when they are resting.

You should also consider having a collar that has a few contact points for your dog because this is essential to having the most consistent training with this kind of collar. It is easy to feel like your dog has a high pain threshold, and that is why they are not feeling anything that you do with the collar. This is not the case, and often the problem is going to lay with the contact points that you have in the collar you purchased.

Often, it is easy to solve this kind of problem if you have a collar that can change up the contact point based on whether your dog has a coat that is short, medium, long, or extra thick. With a short to medium-haired dogs, you are going to be fine with a contact point that is already in the e collar when you purchase it. But what works for these dogs will not work as well with those that have long or thick coats because they just won't be able to feel it.

The short points of contact can be a great option to work with if you have a dog that includes Great Danes, Boxers, English Bulldogs, French Bulldogs, Bull Terriers, and all of the bully breed dogs. The medium contact point is going to work the best for options like Border Collies, Labrador Retrievers, and Goldendoodles. The longer contact points will work with some dogs like German shepherds, golden retrievers, and Rottweilers.

Then if you are working with some of the dogs that have a really thick coat, such as Akitas, Great Pyrenees, and the Bernese Mountain Dogs, then you will want to go with the thick coat contact. And finally, an extra-long contact point is going to work for dogs like the Newfoundland.

You have to take a look at the kind of dog you are working with and then go from there to figure out which kind of contact point is going to be the best. You do not want to go with the long contact point on a dog breed that is a bit smaller and who doesn't have a lot of hair because this is going to be too much for them and can cause pain. But if you have a dog that has more hair or is bigger, the longer points are better to make sure that they will even feel the shock collar when it is in use.

In addition, most of the contact points that are found with these collars are going to be made out of surgical grade stainless steel. The reason that this is used is that this kind of material is not going to rust or corrode away, even if your dog is in a saltwater kind of condition. Make sure that you pick out a collar that meets with this because it will ensure that you are going to be able to use the device for some time.

If you put the electronic collar on your dog and you notice that the neck of the dog seems to be irritated, go through and double-check that the contact points from the collar are stainless steel. If these points are made out of this material, and you notice that the irritation is still there, you can get a contact point that is hypoallergenic and made out of titanium.

The issue of your dog's neck getting annoyed with the contact points is going to be rare, but there are some dogs that are going to be slightly allergic to the small amount of nickel that is found inside of the stainless steel with these contact points, so if they do get irritated, then you just need to pick out a covering that will help to make their skin not come in contact with the stainless steel, and the nickel that it contains at all.

Picking out the e collar that is going to work for your dog requires you to have a good understanding of your dog and how they are going to respond to it. You need to be prepared to spend a bit more because this will ensure that you get a collar that is actually going to work, one that is going to not cause any issues with your dog, and one that will be a great addition to the training regimen that you do while allowing the dog to actually feel the shock or the vibration from the collar. Following some of the tips in this chapter and double-checking that the collar has the right accessories can make things so much easier.

Chapter 4: Properly Fitting the Collar on Your Dog

The next thing that we need to take a look at is the idea of getting the collar to fit your dog just right. You don't want to let the collar get too tight, or the current from the shock will be too much, and the contact points are going to rub and irritate the dog. But if you end up not getting the collar tight enough, then it is not going to phase the dog at all when they do something that sets it off. This is a careful balance that you need to work on to ensure that your dog is going to be comfortable while also making sure that they are going to be able to feel the training method that you use.

The two most common mistakes that a dog owner can make when they get started with this kind of training is that they don't use the right contact points for the collar, and they don't end up fitting the collar onto their dog in the proper manner. The stimulation that the e collar is going to deliver is going to be similar and will feel in a similar manner, as chiropractors like to use for muscle rehabilitation. This means that if the collar is not reaching the right kind of contact with the muscles of the dog, then the stimulation that they experience will be inconsistent.

Another common mistake that some pet owners are going to do is that they put the collar down, so it is too low on the neck of the dog. This is not a good idea because of the shape of your dog's neck. The dog is going to be bigger at the base of their neck, or lower down, compared to at the top of the neck. So, if you end up placing this collar, so it is at the base of the neck when your dog is outside playing around outside, the collar will go up the neck and will lose the snug fit that it had at the start.

The good news is that many of the collars out there are going to tell you what kind of dog breed you are able to put the collar on, so you can get a good idea of whether this is going to work for your dog or not. Always look at the description or ask the company directly to figure out if a particular collar is big enough or small enough for your dog.

Once the collar gets to your home, there is going to be a bit of adjusting that you can do with the collar. This is when you will use the two-finger rule to make sure that the collar fits your dog properly. Most collars are going to have some kind of range of the types of dogs it will fit, so you will have to figure out how to use this and to get the electronic collar to fit well on your dog so that it works in the proper manner.

So, get the collar up on the neck in the right position, and then tighten it up to where you think it needs to go. Then, slide two fingers in and see if it is going to fit or not. If you can fit more than two fingers in there, then the collar is too loose, and you need to tighten it a bit more. If you can't get the two fingers in there and one finger barely fits, then it is time to loosen it up so that it doesn't cause discomfort to the dog.

A good place to help you with referencing where to place this is to cinch the collar down so that you are able to slip in two of your fingers underneath the collar strap on the back of the neck of your dog. Some of the steps that you can follow to make sure that you get this kind of collar to fit on your dog in the proper manner will include the following:

1. Make sure that before you put the collar on at all that the right contact points are already present. For example, if your dog is allergic to nickel and you know this ahead of time, make sure that the right attachments are placed on it before using.

2. De-shed the neck of the dog if they happen to have a coat that is a bit thicker.

3. Place the collar so that it ends up higher on the neck of your dog.

4. Do not place the collar on the top of the neck of your dog. You can pick either the right or the left sides of the dog are fine.

5. Tighten the collar so that it is to a snug fit on the dog. You can tell that it is a snug fit when you can fit two fingers under the collar. This makes sure that it is close enough that your dog will be able to feel it but loose enough that it isn't causing irritation and pain to the dog.

6. Be sure that if the dog is wearing this collar for a long period of time, you should rotate it around every two hours or more. This makes sure that no irritation shows up with the collar.

7. It is often recommended that when the e collar is on, you should not attach a leash to the dog either.

As we just mentioned, it is best if you do not attach the leash to the dog when they have this collar on. The Martingale collar can be a great option to use during training, and they are inexpensive while being easy to find at any pet store in your area. Any harness or collar that you want to use to attach your leash is just fine. Your goal here is to make sure that they are the right size for the kind of dog you have and that they can be fitted tightly to the neck of the dog.

The martingale collar is going to end up tightening if the dog tries to back out of the collar, which is why a lot of dog trainers like to work with it to get the dog to behave the way that they should. If your dog is able to back their way out of the collar, then the martingale collar is the best option to eliminate the chance of this happening when you are trying to train the puppy on how to behave with the collar.

With that said, it is best if you are able to either slip the e collar off your dog before you use the leash or put on the harness or another type of collar and then hook up the leash to that one. Hooking the leash so that it is on the e collar is just going to cause problems. The dog could get out of it, the movements they do while on the leash may make the collar go off without any need to, and it could make things more difficult when you are doing the training process with your dog.

It is much better to work with the e collar as a training tool, and then when you are ready to go on a walk with the dog, or you want to work on some other form of training, take the collar off. It is best to not leave this kind of collar on more than you need. This helps the dog to get a break from using this kind of collar and ensures that you are not leaving it on for too long.

Remember that the collar is just meant to be a training tool and not something that your dog wears all of the time. And once they get more adjusted to the collar and stop doing the behavior that you got the collar for in the first place, then it may be time to stop using the collar any longer.

The final thing that we need to take a look at here is the idea of safety. Your goal here is to use the collar as a way to safely and effectively train your dog to behave the way that you want, not to harm them or cause them any kind of pain. Following the right safety procedures will ensure that you can meet both of these goals in no time.

If you ever have it where the dog is going to need to keep the collar on for more than a few hours at a time, make sure that you do some rotating of the collar after a few hours. So, if the collar is on for eight hours, you will need to move it around three or four times. Moving it from left to right or from right to left is just fine for this process.

You may find that some dogs are going to be able to wear the collar in the same spot for a longer period of time, and other dogs will need to change the position around the neck on a more frequent basis. You have to learn what seems to work the best for your dog, but starting out with a rotation after two hours of the collar is a good place for you to start and helps you to at least move the collar a few times throughout the day.

Also, if your dog is going to swim anywhere, then it is usually a good thing for you to take the collar off them completely. This allows them to get a break and ensures that the collar will be fine. Most of these collars are going to be waterproof, so if they jump into a pool or something without you being able to catch them, the collar will be fine. But it is best if you are able to take it off and give the dog a break, and then allow the neck of the dog to dry off all the way before you try to put the collar back on.

Any time that you need to wash the e collar, make sure to use some warm and soapy water. You should try to wash this on a bi-weekly or so basis to make sure that nothing gets on the collar and causes issues. If it needs to be done more often because your dog likes to make some messes, then this is fine as well. Give the collar some time to dry off after the cleaning before putting it back on the neck of your dog.

You need to make sure that the collar is going to fit your dog properly, and you are able to get it to work on them without causing any irritation or other issues. This is something that takes a bit of practice and some knowledge about your dog. But once you are able to pick out the right kind and get it fitted in the right manner, you are going to see how great this training tool can be to help your dog learn the behaviors they are allowed to use and the ones that you want them to stop doing now.

Chapter 5: Off-Leash Training with the E Collar

Now that we have the right collar for your dog and you have had some time to try it on and get it nice and fitted, it is time to work on a bit of off-leash training with your puppy. Before we decide to transition off the leash with the dog, there are four major pillars that all dog owners need to know to make this process a bit easier, including:

1. Where the stimulation is going to come from.

2. How to turn the stimulation on.

3. How to turn the stimulation off

4. How to avoid stimulation in the first place.

It is common for well-meaning dog owners to rush the training process with the e collar without taking the time to properly train their dog without the collar. Rushing this process often seems like the best option, and whether you are excited to try out some new training with your dog or you just want to get the process done, it is going to be a bad decision for both your dog and for you in the long term.

When an owner decides to rush the process, they are almost always going to be really frustrated with the dog, and they decide that training the dog has to be done now, whether or not the dog is ready for it or not. It is tempting to skip a few steps along the way, but let's follow all of these steps so that you can do right by your dog. And always remember that the training we will do is not just for the dog, but also for you as the dog owner.

Let's stay with the first three days of training. During this time, your goal is to just do two quick sessions a day. You can do one in the morning and one in the evening inside of your apartment or home. And keep the training sessions pretty short. Five minutes up to ten at the most, depending on how your dog is responding to the training. Some people find that their dog is motivated by food, so doing the training for a few minutes before feeding them can help you out with the training.

If you decide that this is the method to use, you can give your dog a small amount of food for each repetition during the training session until the meal is all done. Other times using the treats can be a good motivation as well. You can pick any treat that you want, as long as it is a favorite of your dog, so they will be motivated to listen and do what you want.

First, we need to stop and determine which method you would like to use in order to get the attention of the dog with the e collar, the tone, or the vibration. When we start to progress off-leash and work at long distances, this step will prove to be of benefit and will be paired together with the recall command of "come."

This method of prompting is going to depend on the model of the collar that you use and the company that makes it. If you have a collar that is able to give an audible tone, you will need to use the tone. If the collar has a vibration, then we need to use that. Then there are some collars that will offer you both options and if this is the case, working with the tone is the best because some dogs are going to start feeling scared of the vibrate setting, and this is going to slow down the progress that you are making with the process.

The next thing to work on here is to train on the e collar and the remote and then making sure that you are able to get the collar to fit in the proper manner around your dog's neck. You will begin with the session inside of your house, using a regular six to eight-foot leash on the dog. Tell them to come, and then tap the T/V button as you walk away from the dog. Say 'Yes,' and then give the dog some food or a treat and some praise for doing what you say for coming to you.

If this is working the way that it should and the dog is paying attention to the command that you are giving, then you will notice that the dog will start to follow you around the room. You can also try out with a few other commands, but remember that this session for the first few days should only last for a few minutes, five tops, so you will need to end it pretty quickly.

When the training session is done, make sure that the dog gets a lot of praise and attention. Praise them when they come to you and for doing so well with following you around or doing any other command that you would like to use. This may seem a bit silly, but the more praise that you give, and the bigger deal that you give for the work, the more that the dog will associate the T/V with something that brings them lots of good things.

It is important for you to only work with the e collar for these first lessons for days one to three. Then we will move on to the second part. For days four to seven, you are going to stick with the two sessions per day for a bit longer. These lessons, though, are going to move from the inside to the outside, often in the yard or when you take the dog on a leash walk. Keep the sessions pretty short, not going more than seven minutes for this one.

What we are going to work with over these days is going to help cover many of the teaching points that will help to prepare your dog for the off-leash control that you want to have later on. It is also going to make sure that your dog is going to know the four pillars of e collar training that we talked about before so that they will listen to what you have to say.

Every time that you get started on a new lesson, you should start out by finding the e collar working level for your dog. This has to be done each time, even if it is on the same day, to make sure that the level is never too high or too low for your dog. Think of the working level as the lowest point that your dog is going to feel while still showing you a slight response that they feel this stimulation. It is nowhere near strong enough for them to feel pain or get harmed, but it is definitely strong enough to get their attention.

So, how do we make sure that we are able to find this working level? A good place to start is to practice finding your own working level. Place the collar so that it is on your hand and start the stimulation at the first level. Then give the button a tap. Then go up one level at a time until you start to feel a bit of tingling in your hand. This is going to be the working level of the e collar for you. You now have to figure out when this is happening for your dog, and it is most likely going to be at a different level than what you feel. Make sure that your sessions always start out by finding this level to make things a bit easier and to ensure the training session will be successful.

How to Find the Initial Level

There are a lot of behaviors that your dog is going to show when they are wearing this collar, and they start to feel some of the stimulation. The most common response that you are going to see is your dog looking around them like there is a bug that has landed on their neck or on their head. There are some dogs that may just stop what they are doing right now and look confused. And some dogs will not really show a change other than a bit of muscle twitching on their neck (this is the most common with the bully breeds). Another sign of this is that the dog is going to lick their lips or do other subtle signs along the way.

Each dog is going to respond to the whole e collar thing in a different manner, and it is your job to figure out the best way that your dog is going to respond. Starting at the lowest level and moving up slowly, watching for any kind of sign can be another way to make sure that you pick out the right kind of stimulation that works for your dog.

You can start out with a level on the collar that is 1/100, and then tap the continuous button once quickly and then watch for a slight change to show up in the behavior of your dog. Continue going up to two, and then three, and so on until you start to see a sign from your dog, including some that we talked about above. When you find this level, then you know that this is the perfect level to start the lesson.

With this, you need to restart the process each time. This makes it easier for you to find the level that is perfect for your dog, no matter what time of day or even what day it is. And always slowly build up from the bottom. It is easy to assume that your dog is not going to be able to feel the lower levels of the stimulation, but there are some dogs that are going to feel it at really low levels, and making sure that they aren't getting harmed by starting way up at the highest points can be critical to your success with this.

Now that you know the right stimulation levels for your dog, it is time to start with some of the training sessions for these second set of days. Start by walking your dog in the yard, or even on the sidewalk that is right in front of your home.

Once you see that the dog starts to fixate on something that is in front of you, and they start to get close to pulling on the leash, you can stop, say come, and then tap the T/V button. If the dog looks a bit confused, you want to encourage them to walk to you and walk away while enticing them with a treat. Be sure that you offer some praise and a treat of some kind when they do end up coming to you.

It is possible that the dog is going to become too distracted by the smells and the sights of the outdoors, and you may need to move on to the continuous stimulation button at the level that works on the e collar for your dog. This may get their attention a bit more so that they will decide to listen to you rather than going after the object that has gotten their attention.

As you progress in the training lessons, you may find that you will need to slightly increase the level of stimulation on the collar. This is common as the dog gets more used to the feeling and decides that they are able to ignore it and not listen to what you want them to do. Never jump up more than one level at a time when you are doing this because it could harm the dog, and you often need a lower level than you think.

Once we are to this point, it is time to move on to the training that is needed for days seven to twelve. You are going to work on pretty much the same ideas that we focused on in the last section, but your recalls are going to become increasingly difficult by incrementally adding in more distraction and distance. You will use a long leash for this one, and if you are able to find one that goes up to fifteen or more feet, this can make the process a bit easier. Remember that your end goal here is to take the dog off the leash, so you need them to pass a few tests before you are able to do this.

With these sessions, you need to get the work done outside. You can then increase the session a bit longer here, and instead of just focusing on the five minutes, you can increase it up to thirty minutes to make sure that the new skills that you are teaching to the dog will stick. Two sessions a day is going to work with this as well.

Before you get started with this kind of training, make sure that the collar fits the dog well. Then turn it on, attach the long leash, and make sure you have lots of food and treats ready to help. Start your dog out with an easy lesson by putting something that your dog is going to like in the yard before you even take the dog outside. Plant four or five of these in different areas and then take the dog out for a walk, allowing them to smell around but don't allow them enough room to go and get them.

Find the right level on the collar for the dog and then tell them to "come' when they start to go towards the hot dog and tap on the T/V button. If you find that the dog isn't coming right to you, then hold down on the continuous button for one to two seconds and start walking in the other direction. If your dog does come to you, even if it took a few seconds, make sure to give them lots of praise and a treat for listening.

Because the distraction is pretty strong in this one, you may have to work for a

bit. If the dog decides to ignore the first-come command and the T/V and then

they also decide to ignore the continuous button, it is time to slowly increase the

level of the e collar until they avoid the hot dogs and decide to start walking along

with you. Once they do this, you can shower them with praise and give them the treats or the food that you brought with you. Then move on to the next hot dog distraction and continue on with the same thing until all of it is done or 30 minutes have passed. You will find that your dog will quickly learn that they can avoid the stimulation that you send over just by focusing on you and coming when they hear the tone or feel the vibration.

The most important thing to remember here is to give your dog a lot of praise along the way. If the only part of the training that you are doing is the stimulation to get them away from the distraction, the process is going to be slow, and you are not going to get the results that you want. You want to make the dog feel like coming to you, and leaving the distraction alone is way more worth it than the distraction. And the best way to do that is to add in the stimulation that they don't want with a lot of good praise, which they do want.

This positive reinforcement is something that you want to pay attention to with any kind of training that your dog is doing with you. This is basically when you reward the dog for all of the good behavior that they do with praise, treats, and other rewards of your choosing. This helps them to learn quickly what you want them to do, and because they want to please you, they are going to remember those good behaviors and the treats and rewards that they got for them much faster.

When you are able to couple together the positive reinforcement with the stimulation from the collar, you will find that the dog will quickly learn that going after the distraction on a walk is not worth it. If they just follow you, they can avoid the stimulation while getting a treat and lots of praise along the way. And for most dogs, this is going to be much more rewarding overall, and they will learn quickly.

Each dog is going to be a bit different. Some will need higher levels of stimulation to get them to listen. Some may take a few weeks to learn how to walk around with you without a leash. And some are going to be more stubborn, and you will just have to add in some more consistency in order to get them to follow along with you. But if you use the right level of stimulation, and you make sure that you add in a ton of positive reinforcement for your dog, they will get them off the leash training down.

And those are the steps that you need to use in order to train your dog to walk off the leash. Over time, you will be able to take the e collar off and still get the dog to listen to you and follow along without any leash, just lots of praise and maybe a few treats. It does take at least a few weeks to get this down, especially if your dog is prone to following distractions. But it can really make walks more enjoyable and helps to make sure that the dog learns how to listen to you and follow your commands, no matter where you may take them.

Chapter 6: Perimeter Training with the E Collar

Now that we have had some time to look at how to train your dog to follow you without a leash and without running off to any of the distractions that come up along the walk, it is time to work with some perimeter training with the dog. There are a lot of people and dog owners who get this kind of collar to help keep the dog in their backyard, even if there is not a good fence up in place and ready to use. You can let the collar do some of the work on its own, but you need to be present during this training to make sure that the dog will know exactly where they are allowed to be.

Just like with some of the other types of training that you do with this collar, perimeter training needs to be done after you have had a chance to set up the initial foundations of commands and training with your dog. This means that they should know at least a few basic commands so that they know how to behave when you work on this.

There are two options that you are able to work with when it comes to perimeter training. You can do it with the e collar, or you can choose to do it with a perimeter containment system. Both of these work on a similar idea as one another, but you will find that it is going to have a little different setup.

First, let's take a look at the perimeter training when you decide to use the e collar. Some of the strengths that you will find by choosing this option over the other includes:

1. You will not have to purchase any additional systems or items to do this if you already own an e collar for the dog.

2. This gives you the ability to be more subtle with the training if you are using an e collar with 100 levels.

3. You will get the ability to correct some of the dirty thoughts that the dog could be thinking when it comes to challenging the boundary.

4. You get to be in control of quickly stopping the stimulation if the dog challenges the boundary and is confused about what they need to do in order to make it stop.

5. You get the ability to make sure your dog will be perimeter trained on more than one property without having to get a containment system for each one.

There is a weakness with this one. If you use the e collar to train the dog on where they are supposed to stay all of the time, then you will be responsible for watching the dog more during the training period. You will be the one responsible for bringing the stimulation on, and if you are not there, then the dog can just walk over the line without any repercussions and will run off without you.

This is not necessarily a bad thing. The more that you can be involved in any kind of training that you do with your dog, even with this kind of collar, the better it is for everyone involved. You should be present to watch the dog and make sure they learn the boundaries that they can roam in, and the e collar forces you to do just that.

The other option that you are able to work with when training your dog how to follow their boundaries is going to be the perimeter containment system. This is a system that is put in place like an electric fence almost and will be set up by you to say how far the dog is able to roam. When the dog gets close to the perimeter, the system is going to start sending out the stimulation to tell the dog to move away. There are a few benefits that come with using this kind of system for perimeter training, including:

1. This one is always going to be consistent because the machine is going to be able to turn the stimulation on and off for your dog each time they get close.
2. It gives you the ability to use more of your property, like the sides of the property that are sometimes a bit harder to self-monitor.

There are some weaknesses that come with using this method, of course. The biggest one is that you will need to get an additional unit set up, and then you need to go through and install it properly. Most perimeter containment systems are not going to provide you with a lot of levels of stimulation that they can promise. Most of these are just going to have between three to six levels, and this makes some of the subtle training that you need a bit harder to do. And if you have more than one property that you want to train the dog on with perimeter training, it is much harder with the containment system.

Now it is time to dive right into some of the steps that you can use with perimeter training. This is going to be day one to three with your dog, and we are going to focus on using the e collar for the best benefits. Your first step with this is to put on the collar and attach it to a standard leash. Find the working level that is the best for your dog, and then begin by walking your dog up to the rope. As you walk past the line, you will find that most dogs are going to try jumping over the rope to continue walking along with you.

If this does happen with your dog, hold down the continuous button, and walk the dog back onto the perimeter and then release the button. You may have to do a few repetitions of this one, but soon the dog is going to catch on. Continue with this ten to fifteen times, without saying anything when the dog passes the line or goes back. We want to get the dog to believe with this one that the stimulation turned on because they passed the line, not because of anything that you are doing.

Using verbal commands or praise when the dog goes on either side of the line may seem like the best thing to do, but then you are going to bring in a new challenge later on. If you do this, the dog is going to think that you were doing the stimulation. And once you go inside, or the dog thinks that no one is actually watching them, then they are going to challenge the line and could end up running off.

Once you have been able to get your dog to understand the concept, and they won't go past the line even when you do, it is time to move on to the second step for this training. This should be done within a few days, so if your dog is still being stubborn or struggling, go ahead and increase the collar level and then try again. To know that you are ready to move on to the next step, you should be able to walk across the line with your dog, still on the leash, and have them stop at the line every time, without you doing any commands.

At this point, it is time to start taking the dog to other areas of the yard and see if you are able to follow the same process. You can switch over to the long leash and allow the dog to drag it with them. If you find that the dog tries to follow you rather than staying in the perimeter, then you need to hold down on the continuous button, then release it once the dog goes back, on their own, behind the line.

During this process, be willing and able to help your dog with the leash if you feel like they are getting confused, but the goal is to get them to do this all on their own, without any commands from you. Do this five to ten times, or until the dog catches on, in all the areas of your yard.

Then we are going to move on to day four to seven of the perimeter training. When we get to this stage, you can try adding in some distractions that could show up on the other side of your boundary line. You may even want to work your way up so that at some point, your dog is going to see other dogs that walk by your property. Start out with a lower working level and then increase as is needed depending on the distraction that you see.

After you get through about three weeks of this, keeping the dog within the perimeter that you set, without any commands and just the stimulation helping out, you will be able to remove the visual boundary if you would like. When you see that the dog is doing a good job with this without much help at all, then take off the long leash and continue to add in more distractions to double-check the reliability of your dog and to make sure that they are not going to run away from you.

This process is one that takes some time. You are trying to teach your dog to stay in the yard, where you are able to see them, despite distractions and an urge to just run free. And you are doing this with a collar, rather than with a physical barrier that is going to stop them. Your dog is going to need a few weeks or more to get accustomed to this process and to learn where their boundaries are. But if you do this in the right manner, and you learn how to take your time with the process of training with the e collar, you will find that you can get your dog to stay in the designated area, no matter where you go, and even with a lot of distractions and no physical boundaries, like a fence, there to make them stay put.

Chapter 7: When to Use Commands and When Not to Use Commands

When we get to this part of the training process, you want to make sure that you add in the collar some more so that they can get used to having it on. Additionally, this allows you to begin to stop any bad behaviors that your dog has. This could include things like pulling on the leash, jumping on people, or a lot of excessive barking.

In the beginning, the e collar may be on the dog more than it isn't. As long as you are careful with the levels that you are using it, and you remember to turn the collar around on a regular basis so that it doesn't irritate the skin of your dog, this is going to be fine. And if you are effective with your training methods, you will be able to use the collar for a few weeks or so and find that your dog will be trained to act the way that you want, with none of the negative behaviors.

Remember back to when we were talking about the four pillars from before. These are so important when it comes to training your dog on the e collar, but now we are going to break from tradition a bit and tell you to slightly break away from these four pillars. Trust that this is going to work at getting us to take the training up to the next level for the best results.

One important thing to remember about training your dog is that all good dog training works when the owner is present. Great dog training works even if the owner is not present. There are going to be times when you are not present, and you still want the dog to behave. If you go on vacation and someone stops by to feed and walk the dog, you don't want them to jump all over the person. After perimeter training, there will be times when you want to let the dog outside to play and run around without having to physically be out there with them, making sure that they behave.

And that is where we are going to start out with this chapter. Let's unpack some of the commands and behaviors that we want to use vocal commands for. In the last chapter on perimeter training, we talked about how you did not want to use commands. This is due to the fact that you want the dog to follow the boundary, whether you are there or not. But then, with off-leash training, we did use a command. Learning when to work with the commands and when they are not necessary can make a difference.

Sometimes, you will use the e collar to help with training, and you will want to use some command to go with it. Commands including drop it, go to bed, down, leave it, heel, and come are going to be used in a way that indicates something that you would like the dog to do. Let's call these commands, to make things a bit easier, action commands. These commands are going to be given in a vocal command because it helps the dog learn what we would like them to do.

Then there is the other side of things. This is going to include the moments where we are not going to give commands like the ones before. These behaviors are going to be known as automatic avoidance behaviors. When a dog commits these behaviors, you will not want to give them any verbal cues because they already know that when they feel the continuous stimulation that they can stop that feeling by doing the opposite behavior. If you have trained the dog right, a command is not necessary because they will just do the action that stops the stimulation.

When we try to use some commands to help with stopping these behaviors, some dogs are going to try and cheat the system a bit when they notice that you are not around to watch. For example, if you tell your dog not to jump on people when they are at the door, even if you used the e collar to help with this training, it may not work. It is possible that the moment someone walks into the door early when you were not expecting them, the dog is going to jump on them because you were not there to use the command word of NO JUMPING.

Of course, this is not what we want to have happen. You want to make sure that the dog learns that they are not allowed to do some of these behaviors, whether or not you are around to witness them doing these behaviors. And that is why there are some training sessions where you will avoid all commands and only work with the collar instead.

When you train the dog that they are going to feel a shock or the stimulation each time that they jump on someone who comes through the door (or does some other behavior that you don't approve of), without any command, then they are going to learn to stop doing that behavior as quickly as possible. Even when you are not there to stop them, they will know that if they jump on the other person who comes through the door, there is a big possibility that they are going to get the stimulation, and they do not like that.

But they learn it the other way as well. If they get stimulation when they jump on another person, but they avoid the stimulation by not jumping on the other person, what choice do you think the dog is likely to make? If the e collar training went well, the dog will choose to sit quietly (though they may be wagging their tail excitedly) when someone walks through the door in order to avoid the stimulation.

Using commands when you are trying to stop bad behaviors is not necessarily a bad thing, and it does work. But you will find that the e collar training without the command in most cases is going to be more effective, especially when it comes to times when you just can't be present to stop the negative behavior from happening.

When you are trying to figure out whether you should add in a command or not, figure out whether you want to have the dog stop the behavior when you are there, or if you want to make sure that the dog is always acting in a certain manner, whether you are there or not.

When you take the dog on a walk, and you want to make sure that the dog is going to stay near you and not run away, a command is going to be just fine. You are going to always be there when the dog is walking, so having a command to get their attention and to give them a chance to return back to you before using the stimulation makes sense. Any time that you are working with a command like this, then you can go ahead and come up with a clicker word or another phrase that will tell the dog that it is time to listen to you.

On the other hand, there are some actions that you want to make sure the dog is always following, whether they can see that you are near to them or not. When you are working on perimeter training, and you want the dog to stay in the designated area, or you are working on making sure the dog doesn't jump on others whether you can make it to the front door quickly enough or not, then teaching the dog how to behave with the e collar, and without any command, is going to be better. This teaches the dog that it is the collar that is telling them to stop, rather than the owner, and they will worry about how to behave whether you are near or not.

No matter how much you love your dog, you don't want to spend all day watching them and making sure that they behave. You want to have them behave whether you are around to watch or not. With the right use of the e collar in the training process, you will find that this is easier to do, and it won't be long before you are able to get the dog to listen to you and to follow your rules, whether or not you are around to control the behavior.

Chapter 8: Forms of Correction with Your Dog

As you are working with any training method, whether it is with the e collar or some other method, you need to have some idea in place on how you are going to correct the course of your dog, especially when they are really not listening to you. Think of correct as a way for you as the dog owner to correct the course that your dog is on when the dog is about to jump on someone when they are running across the yard to get away, or when they are ignoring some command that you are trying to give.

Corrections can come in a lot of different forms. You will find that these can be verbal in nature, but it is also possible to get them to work more effectively when you pair them with a physical reminder of some kind. This is where the e collar is going to come in. Your collar level for corrections, if you choose to use it in this manner, is going to be somewhere between the low and medium levels. However, there are going to be times when you need to increase this quite a bit depending on the kind of dog you are dealing with and the situation that is at hand.

Let's take a moment to unpack the three types of correction that you are going to be able to use, and then we will look at the concept of punishment. We do not condone using the e collar as a form of punishment with the dog, and more forms of punishment, whether they are with the e collar or not, are going to be ineffective and can turn the dog aggressive. We will talk more about that in a bit, but first, we need to focus on the three main types of correction that you can use the e collar for, and these include:

1. Low-level suggestions
2. Medium level suggestions
3. High-level deterrents
4. Punishment

You, as the dog owner, have to decide what level of intensity you are going to work with based on the behavior and how much you want the dog to listen to you.

For example, if the dog is just ignoring you, or they temporarily fix the behavior before going right back to it, then you will want to work with a low-level suggestion. If your dog is about to run away or go into the street of an oncoming car, though, then you may want to use the medium level nudges or even the high-level deterrents to get them to stop right in their tracks rather than continuing with the action.

Many trainers like to promote the idea of using just the low-level e collar training with the dog when you need to work with them. This is a terminology that may show up with many companies selling this kind of collar because it is easy to sell the concept to a dog owner who is a bit hesitant about using this training technique at all. But it is not the whole story.

While some dogs are going to be just fine with the lower levels of the collar, some dogs will have to start out at a higher level of corrections, and if they are done to improve the quality of life for the dog, and to make sure that the dog does not get hurt or into trouble, then the higher level of corrections is what needs to be done. Most of the time, though, these higher levels of correction are going to not be used on pet dogs, and you really should try out the other two levels a few times first. If those two levels don't seem to be working, then it is time to bring in the higher levels to see if that helps.

In some cases, the higher level is going to work the best for some dogs because if the dog figures out that the collar can deliver more than just a slight tingle of stimulation, then it is more likely that they will be stubborn and resistant. You have to again watch what your dog is doing and how they respond to the collar, and sometimes the level has to change based on your location and the situation that you are trying to put the dog through.

As you can see here, though, we have a fourth component that goes with this, the idea of punishment for your dog. When you are training your dog, punishment is not highly recommended at all, and you should only use it if you find that absolutely nothing else is working or when there are going to be some big implications for the safety and the health of the dog if they choose to not listen to the command.

For example, an owner may choose to use punishment when the dog is charging towards a busy road, ready to chase a dear, or even about to go after a rattlesnake. The punishment is going to be designed to help your dog stop in one stimulation so that they won't do that behavior again. You won't get the luxury of using failed repetition with a rattlesnake like you will with off-leash training or with perimeter training, so the higher amount is used to teach them how to behave fast.

This does not mean that you should go crazy with using this. It is a last-ditch effort to make sure that your dog is going to pay attention to you and that they won't get hurt in the process at all. But other than this, and in the most extreme cases, you do not want to set the level on the collar so high that it is going to hurt the dog. Keeping it at the level that is the most comfortable for your dog while still getting their attention on you and doing what you want is the most important thing here.

The difference that is going to happen between a high-level correction and a punishment will be the duration of the stimulation. When you use the high-level correction, you are going to do a quick pressure on a higher level, but only if your dog seems to respond to that rather than some of the other levels from your collar.

With a punishment, you may have it at a slightly higher level than normal, and you will hold onto it for two or three seconds to really get the attention of the dog, so they stop and listen to you. Always remember to not use the high-level corrections or the punishments too prematurely. Often the dog is going to listen to you at one of the lower levels, so working with that is the most effective and will make sure that the dog does what you want without getting harmed in the process.

Chapter 9: What If My Dog Faces Some Distractions

Wouldn't it be nice if you could use the collar just a few times, and then your dog would be fully trained, and not even the biggest distraction in the world would be enough to get them to stop behaving? This is a fantasy that you may hope for when you get started with some of the work that we do with this guidebook, but it is not really the reality that you will get to enjoy.

Dogs, as well as most humans, are going to face distractions at some point in their lives. And in the beginning, when the dog is younger and trying to explore and learn about new things, the distractions are going to make it harder to train them. Your goal is to work on minimizing the distractions and getting the dog to follow your commands and your rules even if there is a big distraction coming their way. But in the meantime, before the training is complete, distractions are something that you have to plan for and train against to make the collar training effective.

Reliability in your dog is critical when it comes to training the dog for some pretty obvious reasons. E collar training can be a good way to develop some trust that only seeing can make you believe in. Many dog owners are worried about using this kind of collar to get their dog to behave the way that they want, and they feel that by doing this kind of training or relying on this kind of method, they will end up hurting the dog, turning the dog into an aggressive animal, or not seeing any results in the process.

But working with the e collar is one of the best ways that you can truly get your dog to obey your rules, no matter where you are in the training process or even what kind of dog you have. Sure, there are some dogs that are more persistent and stubborn than the others, and you may have to take some more time to work with them to get them to listen to you. But over time, with the right use of the e collar, and some other training methods thrown in as well, you will find that the collar can develop trust between you and your dog, and you will be able to get them to listen to your commands, even if there are a bunch of distractions going on around you.

The e collar is a great way for you to be in control. And that is basically what all of the other training methods are teaching you to do as well. You don't want to take this overboard and try to harm your dog, but you do want to train them that you are the one in control and that you expect the dog to listen to you and do what you want.

However, there is one truth that we need to explore a bit in this chapter, one that some people are not that comfortable with when they start with e collar training. But it is something that needs to happen so that you can be prepared any time you go out and for any kind of distraction that may get the attention of your dog. And this truth is that when you work with e collar training, at some point, you must go through part of the training and put your dog into positions where they will want to ignore some of the commands that you are given.

If you only work on the collar when there are no distractions, it is easy for the dog to listen to you. They have nothing that takes their attention away, and you are the most interesting person at that moment. This isn't going to be the same when you are at the park, going on a walk, or somewhere else that is away from home. And adding in some of these distractions and training your dog on how to avoid and ignore them before they even show up in real life can ensure that the dog is going to listen and follow you, rather than running off or going after the distraction when you give a command.

This brings up the question about what will be the perfect level to use on this collar when the dog is near distractions that may make them not listen to you. As you work with your dog, you will find that there are three e collar levels that will determine how your dog responds to the shock. It is either not enough, just right, or too high. Of course, these are all subjective numbers, and it will depend on the dog you are working with. A large dog will be able to take more than a smaller dog, for example.

To make these things even more complicated (as if they weren't difficult to work with already), not enough, just right, and too big change not only with each day, but they will also depend on the level of distractions that your dog is around when you do the training. If you get up in the middle of the night and get a drink of water and stub your toe on the way, it is going to feel like it hurts really bad. If you startle up in the middle of the night because you hear that someone is getting into the house, and when you go to check it out, you stub your toe. You still feel the pain, but it won't be as bad, and you can still power through to the back door with the pain.

This is the same kind of idea that is going to happen to your dog when they use the e collar and feel distracted by something. Your dog's pain threshold will change from inside to outside, from low distraction to high distraction, and you have to make sure that you fully understand how this changes and what levels your dog may need based on the level of distraction that is around them at the time that you use the collar.

As you noticed, when you went from training inside to training outside, the threshold that you have to use probably went up. And then when you head outside to do some off-leash training or some perimeter training, when there was a distraction nearby, you will need to up the levels as well. This may seem like a lot of work in the long run, but it is going to ensure that your dog agrees to listen to you, even if something interesting or fun comes across their path and they want to run.

Of course, you do have to make sure that you are not pulling any mental levels in your mind. If you work with a trainer or find that one number was the highest the dog could handle when you did your initial training, don't let this make you stop if you need to. Some dogs will never really need to go above this higher level. But then there are others who will grow more accustomed to the shock and will decide that going for the distraction or jumping up on people is worth it.

If the dog is behaving in this manner, and you refuse to up the collar, then they are going to start getting out of control and will stop doing what you want. Sure, you don't want to hurt the dog, but this is why you go with the working level that we talked about before. Slowly upping it by one small level at a time will help you to see if this is the problem or not. And as soon as the dog starts responding again and stops trying to take control and go against your wishes, you stop at that level and use that instead.

It is easy, though, to assume that the dog will never go above what we had during the training. But dogs change all the time. As they get used to the collar and the shock, or they get bigger and can handle more vibrations, you may have to change up what you are doing. Watch the behavior of your dog and determine if upping the level is necessary or not. If they still respond to you and act the way they are supposed to without going up, then just leave the number where it is. But if they stop listening and see to need it a bit higher, then go ahead and do that as well.

Think of it this way. There are some dogs who are going to be masters of manipulation. This means that if they are able to test you, they will. They like to test you in every way that they can, and if they feel that they are able to do what they want without you increasing the level, or if they see that you start to hesitate a bit to press the button to get them to behave, then you are going to end up with some problems. The dog will see this as you letting up some of the control, and you are going to have more problems down the line.

Your job during this process is to make sure that you provide the dog with distractions, in a controlled environment if you can, before they actually try to run away from you due to the distractions. We have talked about some of the ways that you can do this when we looked at the steps used for off-leash training and perimeter training.

You will start out with training the dog on the e collar without going out of the home. This is also a good training process for you because it ensures that you learn how to work with the collar and that you get used to the working level that your dog can handle. Plus, you can get in more practice with the commands that you have been teaching.

Then you can spend some time outside. Even if you are in the backyard with a fence around you and no added distractions like people or dogs walking around, there will be some distractions that you can work with. The dog will want to jump around and play rather than listen. A bird may fly by. And a million other things will catch their attention. You will have to work with the dog to figure out the right level on the collar to keep their attention and make them listen to your commands the whole time.

Once you have progressed with the backyard, it is time to do some controlled distractions outside of it. You can walk up and down the street in front of your home to get them used to other people. You can even plant some items that you know will get the attention of your dog and then convince them to stay away from those items. These distractions won't hurt the dog if they don't listen right away, but you still want to make it the goal here to just have them listen to you and your commands with the help of the e collar.

When you are ready, it is time for the big challenge. Taking the dog on walks to the park and other places where distractions are going to abound, and making sure that when you want them near you or you give another command, they are going to listen to you. This one will take some time to build up to, but if you are able to do it, then you will see some great results with the training, and worries about the dog running away or getting in harm's way will be gone.

Determining the right level that is needed to help your dog listen to you even when there are a lot of distractions around can seem tough. You, of course, want to make sure that they are going to listen to you, rather than following that squirrel across a busy street or going after someone else they want to play with. But you also have to balance this with not having the levels too high. And since the levels on the collar will change on a regular basis based on the age of the dog, if they are used to the collar, and where you are with the dog, it is going to take a lot of trial and error along the way.

The best thing that you can do to help with this is to work with distractions from the beginning. You can get the dog a bit used to the collar at home, where you know it is safe. But when you are ready, you will be able to take them outside. And introducing them to a lot of different distractions right from the beginning will make it easier.

This helps you to be prepared when you do go out and an unexpected distraction comes up. And it lets the dog know that, no matter what catches their eye and their attention, you are still the one in charge, and they need to listen to you. While there may be some other methods out there that you can use to make this happen and to ensure that the dog is going to listen to you along the way, the e collar is going to be the most efficient method for you to use with this one.

Chapter 10: Common Questions Dog Owners May Ask

Now that we have spent some time laying down the foundation of using this guidebook and how to work with the e collar, it is time to answer some of the questions that a lot of dog owners are going to have when they decide to add this training method to their list of things to work on with the dog. Some of the most common questions that many dog owners like to ask when they are ready to use this collar include:

Will the dog get collar smart?

For the most part, this is not going to be a big issue to worry about. Most trainers will say that if you do a bit of training and laying the groundwork with the commands before you start using the e collar, then the dog is not going to be able to figure out that the e collar is where the stimulation is coming from. However, you will find that if you put the e collar on your dog randomly for three weeks before you even let the unit be turned on, your dog will still get collar smart. Dogs are smart, and they are able to figure out where the stimulation is coming from pretty quickly.

It is pretty much hard to avoid your dog figuring out that the collar is there and that it is the reason they feel the stimulation. It's to be expected that the dog is going to figure out that the collar is the thing that is providing them with the new stimulation, vibration, and tone. However, your job is to get the dog to respond to the requests that you have with the collar, even though they know where the stimulation is coming from.

How long should I let my dog wear the e collar?

There are going to be two key factors that will determine how long your dog should be wearing the e collar. This is going to include the age of your dog and how consistent you are able to be with your training. Younger dogs are going to be on the collar for longer because the world is new to them, and everything is going to be a big distraction to them that they want to explore. These dogs have yet to check everything out, chase after everything, and take it all in. And this makes them a bit harder to train, and you may have to keep the collar on them for longer than an older dog.

As your dog ages and matures, they will find that there are fewer things around to distract them. They will not be as interested in new things, and there will be fewer things that are new to them, which will mean they need less prompting with the e collar, and they won't need to use it as much. And you won't need to keep it on them as much.

Another key factor to consider is the consistency you use with training the dog in the first place. If you are not consistent with the collar, and you are not consistent with what you expect out of the dog and with some of the other training that you do, then you will find the collar will not be as effective, and you will need to put in more work to see results. You will find that there is a direct correlation between the clients who hesitated when they needed to use the collar and the dogs who ended up having to wear the collar for a longer period of time.

You can't let yourself hesitate if you are going to use this training device. Any time that you hesitate to back up the commands that come with the e collar, you are letting the dog know that they have the option to manipulate you if they want. There are options of training that you can use that won't require you to always push the button to get the shock. But if you need to use the button along with the command because the dog is not listening to you, then you should not hesitate to do this.

For example, a good method that you can use to train with this collar is to say the command and give the dog a chance to listen and obey you. But if the dog decides to not listen to the command and doesn't listen to what you say, then you can use the collar. Sometimes turning on the beeping or the vibration first after they ignore the command will be enough to get them to listen and come do what you want. If they are still not paying attention, then you will do the stimulation to get them to stop ignoring the requests and commands that you are using.

You can work with any type of training program that you would like along with the collar, but remember that consistency is key. If you use the collar some days and not on others, or you hesitate when it is time to push on the button, you are going to end up with a mess. Your dog is not going to listen, and you have just taught them that they are able to run the show and do what they want. And this will just make the training a lot harder overall.

How can I transition off using the e collar?

At some point, you may decide that the e collar has done its job, and you want to be able to transition off so that you are no longer using the collar on your dog. The majority of dog owners out there will assume that the collar has done its work too early, and they will then decide to take the collar off their dog too early.

Removing the e collar before the right time can really be detrimental to your goal of having a reliable dog.

It is tempting to take this off too early. You see that your dog is doing well with the collar on. The dog is obeying you and following your commands when you have them on the collar. You assume that this reliability is going to follow as the dog goes off the collar. And then everything goes backward. Your dog sees that the collar is off and doesn't have to respond to the stimulation any longer. And they start going back to their old habits and not listening or following commands any longer.

When this happens, it is a good sign that the dog was not ready to transition off the e collar. You need to make sure that your dog is really ready, and quitting cold turkey is going to be a bad day. The dog is going to instantly notice that the collar is off and that they don't feel the stimulation, and because of this, they are going to start doing what they want.

A better method to work with is known as the 10+15 method. It is a simple way to help you first determine if your dog is even ready to get off the collar, and then it can walk you through the steps that are needed to ensure the dog can actually go off the collar without reverting back to some of their old ways.

If your dog is not out and about wearing the collar, then it is hard to guarantee the reliability that the dog is going to show when it is time to comply with your commands. It is tempting to wean off the collar when you are ready, but before the dog is actually ready at all. But you need to make sure that you and the dog are 100 percent consistent with the training for six weeks or more before you even think about the transition to removing the collar.

After the six weeks have gone by, and the dog is listening to you and following your commands 100 percent of the time, it is time to consider working on the transition phase. Your dog will need to wear the collar for this transition period, so don't think that this is a time to take the collar off and throw a party. Doing this is going to cause them to revert back and can mean that you have to start all of your training over again.

For the first ten days of this method, you will only be giving the T/V with your commands. If your dog can make it through the ten days wearing the e collar and you have not had to follow the commands of the T/V with a correction or any stimulation, then this is a very good sign for your training and for taking the dog off the collar. You can then progress to what is going to happen over the next fifteen days. If you find that there were times when you needed to follow up on the T/V command with corrections, then it is not time to transition off, and you should work with this method of training for longer.

Always go at the speed that is the best for your dog. Some dogs are going to be done pretty quickly, and others are going to need more time to adjust and learn how to use the collar and how to behave. If your dog is not able to get through the full ten days without any follow up with a correction, then this is a sign that you need to stick with the e collar for a longer period of time.

Of course, some dogs catch on quickly, and you may be good at reading when your dog is ready to transition off the collar. If you are able to go for the full ten days without any issues, then you can go for the next fifteen days. During this stage, you are going to continue having the dog wear the collar, but your goal is to eliminate the commands from the T/V.

If your dog can do fifteen days straight without any need of the T/V or of the correction stimulation any time that you give a command, then it is time to leave the collar off the dog and in the closet. If you find that any corrections or even just the T/V are needed during this time, then go back to using the collar for at least a few more weeks or more until they are able to pass this test.

This can seem like it is taking a long time, but you need to make sure that it is something that you focus on. Your collar is your best friend for being able to control your dog and get them to listen to the commands that you give. If you take the collar off too soon, and your dog isn't ready to listen to you all of the time, even without the collar, then you are going to run into some troubles. But if the dog passes your 10 + 15 test, then this is a good sign that the dog has passed the training that you have set up with this collar, and it is time to take the collar off the dog.

How can I use this type of collar if my dog has already worn a perimeter fence collar or a bark collar?

Another thing we need to take a look at is if your dog has used some kind of collar in the past, one that is similar to the e collar, though they may work in slightly different ways. Dogs who have experience with a perimeter collar or a bark collar may find that they need to work with a few extra steps during training before they respond to the e collar training. Some dogs who have had training with the other types of collars are going to be a bit apprehensive about the collar, especially if the previous training they received was not that good. You have to keep this in mind whenever you decide to start some of this training with your dog.

Remember that there is nothing that is inherently positive when it comes to the bark collar, so it is likely that your dog is going to really hate them. However, with the perimeter training, the dogs are less likely to shy away from the collar by itself because most dogs have learned to associate the freedom of being outside and running around with the collar, so they may even be willing to put it on and learn with it.

We first need to take a moment to unpack a few things that you are able to do to make sure this collar training is a positive experience for a dog who may have had a bad experience in the past. The first thing that you should do here is always put a leash on the dog before you put on this collar. And always bring in lots of treats, praise, and other forms of positive reinforcement so that the dog can start to see that this collar, even though they may be apprehensive about it to start, is going to be a good thing.

When you start out with the training, you may need to take an extra week of training before you go with the foundation period that we talked about before. The reason that you need this extra week or so is because you are trying to not only train your dog how to behave with the collar on, but you are trying to convince the dog that this collar is not a bad thing. Because of the exposure that the dog had to the perimeter training or a bark collar in the past, they are going to expect that the low levels on this collar are going to quickly get more uncomfortable because they have an association based on those other tools that were used on them. This is why this additional step is necessary for this kind of dog.

This step is one where you need to pick out a collar that has 100 levels. If you end up with a collar that only has 10 levels, for example, the jumps between levels are going to be too large, and the dog is going to get nervous and won't help you at all with this kind of dog. You want to go with such a subtle level that your dog is hardly going to show that they even feel the stimulation at all. If you "think" that you see the dog feel the stimulation, then this is the right level to use during this stage.

You don't want the stimulation level to be very high here. The dog should feel it, but there should not be any discomfort or anything. We are not training the dog to listen. We are showing them that the collar is not a bad thing and that it won't hurt them to have it on. This gives the dog some confidence and ensures that you are going to be able to see some results when you use the e collar on your dog.

To help you begin with this additional step, you need to do the most subtle e collar working level that is going to work with your dog. Once you have been able to find this level, you can say your dog's name and then tap on the continuous stimulation once. Right after this, you will give your dog lots of praise and their favorite treat. This helps the dog to learn that this collar may seem like one that they were put on in the past, but it is easier on them, and it is a positive thing because of what happens after.

You should consider doing this process when you are able to be outside and even on a walk. You can continue on with the walk, and during it, do this five to ten times or on the whole time. Practice this a few times for the next week before you go through and do some of the foundational training for the e collar, as we looked at earlier.

This adds about a week or so to the training period, but it is the best option to use when it is for a dog that has a bad history with some other similar collars. It helps them to see that there is nothing wrong with this collar and that the lower level is not going to jump up and start causing them any harm at all. This will really make your e collar training easier with the dog, especially if their past experience was bad, and they are really hesitant to work with this kind of collar training.

How much distance between me and the dog will be too much for the collar?

Sometimes your dog is going to be ready to run and can start to get away from you. This is pretty normal, especially when they are a puppy and pretty young. You want to make sure that you are getting a collar that is able to handle a little bit of distance in case the dog starts making a run for it. The description for the collar should say how far it is able to reach.

Some of these collars are going to only be for about half a mile, and this is usually enough. If your dog likes to bounce off quickly, you may want to go with a mile range or higher, but that is meant to work more for a terrain that is hilly or for hunting dogs. You have to determine how far of a range you think that you need for your dog, but it is best if you are able to get one that has at least half a mile on it.

Is the collar going to cause my dog any harm?

The collar in and of itself is not going to harm the dog. It is meant to be a good training tool and can make the dog slightly uncomfortable, but it is not meant to harm the dog. And as long as you make sure to flip it around on occasion, if you plan to leave it on for a long time, then the dog should be just fine with the collar and how it works.

The collar is going to be an inanimate object, and just like any object of this kind, it is going to be subject to the judgment and skill of the one who is using it. If you are not careful with this collar or you decide to work with it as a form of punishment with the dog, then it is possible for you to hurt the dog. When the device is used right, it is not going to hurt your dog at all, and it is going to be a humane and safe tool with a lot of benefits to training your dog.

Think of it this way, though. Even a regular collar and a leash are going to be painful and harmful to the dog if you don't use it the right way, and if you get angry and yank at it too much. Yes, the e collar can be harmful and can hurt some dogs if you turn it all the way up or use it in an improper manner.

But if you choose to work with your e collar in a responsible manner, you will find that it is going to be helpful. There is a bit of discomfort that comes with it when it is at the right level, but this is how you are able to make sure that the dog is going to pay attention and do what you want. The only time that the e collar becomes mean and cruel to the animal is when the owner doesn't know how to use it or chooses to use it in an improper manner.

Will this cause my dog to become more aggressive?

There are some dog owners who are not going to use the collar because they worry it is enough to make their dog more aggressive overall. They feel that if the dog is going to feel the stimulation when they try to do something, then the dog is going to take it out on them or on the collar, and then all of the hard work with the training is going to go out the window.

This is not something that you need to worry about if you choose to work with the collar in the proper manner. If you slowly work up to the right working level on the collar, only use it for training purposes rather than all the time, and make sure that the dog learns that the collar is causing the stimulation and their actions are causing the stimulation, rather than their owner, you should not have to worry about the dog becoming aggressive.

Again, this is going to depend on how the user decides to use the device. If you aren't going to pay attention to what you are doing with the product if you start out at a setting that is too high because you are going to just jump right in without learning about your dog if you make the dog wear the collar all of the time, or you plan to use this as a form of punishment rather than dealing with it as a way to train your dog how you would like them to pay. Use the device properly, and your dog is going to learn how to behave and act the way that you would like. Use it in the wrong manner, and you are going to run into some problems with the behavior of your dog, and the work is going to backfire on you.

Can the collar cause burns?

E collars are going to produce a finely tuned stimulation that feels like it is pulsing. They are not going to be able to produce any heat, so there is no reason that it should be causing any burns on your dog at all. Those who talk about the idea that these collars are causing burns are showing ideas of what happens with pressure necrosis. This only happens when you don't rotate the collar or take it off on a regular basis.

If you are not willing to flip the collar around at regular intervals, and you plan to leave it on for days on end without ever taking it off, then yes, the skin is going to be rubbed raw a bit, and that can be a problem. For those who are responsible owners and who make sure to move the collar around the way that it should, then you will find that the collar is going to work just fine without any kind of burns at all.

Is it really necessary to purchase one of these collars?

This one is going to be a personal preference based on what you would like to do with your dog. There are a lot of different training options that are out there for you to choose from, and for the most part, you will be able to properly train your dog without this method at all. With that said, the e collar can make your life so much easier. You will be able to train your dog faster and get them to listen, even without some commands. And if you need to worry about your dog running off or getting harmed, then this is the collar that will help you to get it done.

When you choose to work with the e collar, make sure that this is not the only method that you choose to use with the training. You first need to be able to establish some of the commands that your dog needs to know, or the dog is going to be confused when you add in the collar. But if you use this collar as a training method, rather than as something that is done on its own, you will find that it is much more successful to your goals.

Is a vibration collar a better choice?

The thing is, you can use a modern e collar and find that it does have the vibration feature built-in. This could be as simple as a tap or a pager. Some owners feel that the vibration is going to be better, but for some dogs and some situations, this isn't going to be true. The vibration, in most cases, is going to have a stronger feel, and to some dogs, it can be jarring and a bit frightening. The stimulation is going to be a sensation that is more subtle, and you can adjust it better than you can with the vibration. This is why having the feature can be nice, but the stimulation is going to be more effective for your training.

A good way to figure out what your dog is going to feel when they wear the collar is to feel it using your own hand first. You can put it on your neck, wrist, or hand, or anywhere else that you would like to get an idea of what the dog is going to be feeling. Just remember here that you are not going to be able to perceive the stimuli in the same way that your dog does.

Some dogs are going to be more sensitive to the stimulation, and you just need to turn down the dial a bit to make it work for them. Then there are some dogs who need it at a higher level before they even start to feel it at all. You have to do a bit of experimenting to figure out the level on the collar that is going to be the best for them so that they feel and notice the stimulation but that it is not going to harm them at all.

Do I need to have a lot of knowledge or a high skill level to use the collar?

Anyone is able to use this kind of collar. You may want to read up on the specifics of your collar based on the company you decide to purchase it from. But if you are responsible when you use the product, and you make sure that you follow the tips in this guidebook, you will find that using the e collar is pretty easy, and you don't need to have any special skills at all.

Is it possible to train my dog how to behave without the collar?

Yes, there are a lot of dogs that are trained without the use of this collar at all. People have been able to train their dogs to follow off the leash, to come when called, and many other commands for hundreds of years without these collars. But the reality is, when this technology was first introduced, it brought many benefits along the way.

The collar is not meant to replace some of the other training methods that you are working with, and it is not the only method that you are able to use. It is the most effective when you combine it together with the foundations of command training ahead of time. If you are able to do this, then you will find that the dog knows what you are talking about when you give them a command and may respond to the stimulation so much faster.

There is always more than one way to reach your goal. But many dog owners find that using the e collar, along with some of the other training methods out there and a strong foundation of commands and training, is a very effective method to help you to train your dog the way that you would like.

It is going to be up to you how you would like to train your dog and whether you want to work with the e collar on your dog or not. Never let the idea that this is going to hurt your dog or make them more aggressive or cause other issues make you stay away from this great training method. If you feel like another method or training tool is going to be the best for you, then that is fine. But keep in mind that the e collar can be a great option for you to work with and will help you to really get your dog trained faster than before.

As you can see, there are a lot of different things that you are able to do when it comes to working with the e collar and all of the neat things that you can train your dog to do with it. But being prepared and knowing the best steps to take when getting started, how to handle it if your dog has had a bad experience with these collars, or other similar ones, in the past, and how to know when it is time to transition off the collar is going to make a big difference when it comes to how well you are able to train your dog using this method.

Chapter 11: Other Problems the E Collar Can Help You Solve with Your Dog

Training your dog to behave in the manner that you would like is something that takes some time and effort. Many people are surprised by how much work they have to put in to help make sure that their dog is going to behave. But the earlier you start with this, and the more consistency that you are able to add into the mix, the easier this process is going to be, and the more likely it is that your dog is going to always listen to your commands.

There are also a lot of different trading methods that you are able to use when it is time to train your dog to listen to what you want. And one of these methods, one that can really help to keep your dog from disobeying and can speed up the process of training, especially if you are using it along with the other training methods out there, is the e collar. This guidebook has taken a look at some of the neat things that you are able to do with e collar training and some of the different commands that you are able to use.

With that in mind, off-leash training, avoiding distractions, and perimeter training are not going to be the only commands that you will ever want to train your dog to do. There are a lot of problems that can come up with your dog that the e collar is able to help out with, as long as you make sure that you use it in the proper manner. Let's take a look at a few of these and explore just how we are able to use the e collar to help us stop these problem areas and get our dog to behave in the manner that we want.

Stealing food off the kitchen counter

While we may love our dogs, we are not going to be too happy that they try to steal some of the food off the kitchen counter when you turn your eyes away. Your dog sees it as a great treat or some food that should be theirs, especially if they are able to reach it, and it is your responsibility as the dog owner to make sure that they avoid the item and don't try to eat it.

Remember, with this one, that when you do decide to tackle this issue, you will not give any commands. If you do try to associate some commands with this one, then the second you leave some food out on the counter and run to the other room, the dog will jump up and get that food item again. You want to make sure that your dog will stop stealing food, whether you are present in the room to watch them behave, or you are in another room.

The steps that you should take in order to make sure your dog knows to never steal food off the counter and that they can only have the food that you provide to them will include:

1. Put your dog in another room for a few minutes. It can be any other room that you are comfortable with. You just need them to be there while you set things up. It is imperative that you don't let the dog see what you are trying to do.

2. When you are ready, put the collar onto the dog, and double-check that it is turned on.

3. Place a small or medium-sized spoon on the edge of your counter and bait it with something that the dog will like. It is best to use something that has

a strong smell to entice the dog, such as a piece of a hot dog or some peanut butter.

4. Select the right level on the collar based on whatever the working level is for your dog inside of the home, and then add about ten levels to it. So, if your dog usually responds in the home to 13/100, you will want to go with 23/100. If your dog is really sensitive to the stimulation that comes with this collar, it is fine to go a lower amount up to fit their needs.

5. When this is set up, let the dog out of the room you left them in. Take the remote with you when you go into a different room other than the kitchen. Do something like work on your computer or watch a movie there.

6. When you hear the spoon hit the ground, you can hold onto the continuous button for a second without saying a word to the dog.

7. After the first correction, wait about half a minute and then go get the spoon. Add on a bit more bait, and then put it back on the counter.

8. You should increase the level up by ten, or what is best for your dog, each time that you need to set the protocol up again until the dog leaves the food alone.

With this one, you do not need to work with any commands at all. If you do use a command, it is going to set you back, and you will end up with a dog who will still take the food. They will just wait until you are away from home or when you can't catch them in the act. Your dog, by this time, already knows that you do not like them stealing food, so now your goal is to follow through with your control to correct this behavior at a time when they think you can't.

The question that a lot of people are going to have with this one is why do they need to start the training at a level that is ten points above the normal working level? The reason for this is that this is one of the situations where your dog will actually be given the opportunity to get something that they want. If you keep the level at a gentle correction, then the dog is not going to be deterred from getting what they want.

The dog wants the food. This is something positive to them, a type of reward to them. And a gentle correction may be uncomfortable a bit, but when it comes to choosing between the discomfort and the great reward of the food, the dog is going to dive right into the food. But when you turn on the collar to a higher level, this is going to become a bigger correction, and the dog is not going to like it.

Now, you may have to go through and up it a few times before you get to the right level to stop the dog. Your goal is to find the level where the dog decides avoiding the discomfort is worth more than going after the treat. When this happens, you will find that the dog is going to stop stealing the food. And if you are able to avoid giving any kind of command when you do this, the training can be quick and efficient, and it won't be long before your dog stops trying to steal food from the counter.

One note to keep with this is that if you are trying to do this training with more than one dog, you may want to get a little camera or use your camera on your computer to help you figure out which dog needs to be corrected each time. Just make sure that it is on mute so that the dog doesn't know that you are on the other side, but it can hurry up the process and make sure that you are getting trained and stop eating food at the same time.

The Dog Eats Poop

If you see that this is happening with your dog, make sure that you talk to your vet to make sure that there are no issues like parasites, incomplete diets, thyroid issues, Cushing's, and diabetes. If the vet has checked out the dog and has eliminated any medical reason that could cause your dog to do this, and you have been able to work on the foundation of training with the e collar, then it is time to work on the steps that are needed to stop this behavior.

After you are done doing the e collar foundation training, it is time to get started. This procedure is not going to need you to use any treats, praise, or even a command because it is an implied behavior. Your goal is for the dog to never do this kind of behavior again.

To start this, you need to have the dog on a long leash. Take the dog out to an area where you already know they are going to find some feces. Start at a level that is ten points above what you usually use with the e collar to start with, and then you can work up from there.

When the dog smells some of the feces and starts to act like they are honing in on the scent, and is about one foot from the feces, hold down on your continuous button for the collar. This should be done for two seconds, but if you find that the dog is not fazed by it and continues on with their intent, then it is time to increase the level. There are some models that you can purchase this collar that allow you to hold down on the continuous button while increasing the stimulation level at the same time.

As you are doing this, make sure that you don't try to say a command. It may come a bit naturally, but remember, you don't want the dog to listen when you use the command, and then go right ahead and do the action when they think that you are no longer watching. If you have a collar that is not able to increase the stimulation level while holding onto the button, you can release the button and then increase the level by ten points (or a point that works for your dog if they are really sensitive to the stimulation), and then re-apply and see what happens.

When your dog does what you want and walks away from the feces, it is your job to act like nothing has happened because you don't want them to think that you are the one causing the stimulation. As you walk away, consider turning the stimulation down a bit before they get to the next spot. This helps the dog to see that the stimulation gets more intense the closer they approach the feces and may help them to stay back and away from the issue.

When you see that your dog starts to avoid the feces rather than walking up to it, you can allow them to be off the leash a bit as you continue to watch them. If you let the dog off the leash and you notice that they still take advantage of this as a new opportunity to not listen to you, you can progress by starting at a higher level. After a few days of practicing this, you will find that your dog will stop approaching the feces, and this problem will be solved.

Jumping Up on People

The next issue that we are going to take a look at is the idea of stopping your dog from jumping on others. This is a big issue. Often the dog is not going to mean to be bad or cause trouble, but they are excited to see someone else, and this is the way that they show the excitement. But it can cause issues. You and others who come to your home may not like the dog jumping up. And if you have someone who is elderly in age that the dog jumps on, it can cause some issues as well with knocking them over.

You will find that the e collar is going to be a great tool to use for this because you can use it to create some distance between those who walk through the door and your dog wanting to jump, and it doesn't require any emotions, so you won't have to worry about that getting in the way. The training that happens with jumping on people will be similar to the training that we have done above, but you will do it in a more nuanced manner because while we want the dog to stop jumping, we still want the dog to be social and comfortable with other people when the training is done.

Whether you are doing this inside the home or off the leash outside, the protocol is going to be the same. You want to set the level of the collar at the chosen working level, and then just increase it a few levels. Allow a friend or someone else you know to come into your home and instruct them that they should ignore the dog for the first few repetitions.

If during this process, you see that the dog is jumping on them, then you need to hold down the continuous button when they jump and then release it once they stop with the jumping. No one, neither you nor the other person coming into your home, should give any command when this is happening because you want the dog to avoid jumping on others whether you are there or not.

You may notice that some dogs are going to be quick jumpers. They are going to jump up on others without much notice, and before you are able to say or do anything, they are all done with the jump. With this kind of dog, you must keep your finger on the button for the collar so that you are ready to push before this big jump happens. In addition, be aware that this kind of dog is more likely to need the level on the collar a bit higher to prevent them from jumping.

Then there are those dogs that like to jump up and are likely to stay there. This process is going to be pretty similar, but you may need to hold down on your button for a bit longer. You can usually go at a lower level as well. In either of the two cases, you may find that the dog decides to ignore you at the lower levels, which means that you will need to do some work to increase the level as it is needed. Remember here, though, that if you do increase the level, and you do it too much, then this will make it so that the dog won't want to approach anyone any longer, and that is definitely not what we are trying to do here.

When you see that your dog is excelling at this kind of training, you can instruct your friend or family member to be a bit more animated with the dog. At this same time, you can put the bowl of treats outside your door for the friend to have access to when they enter, and the dog behaves and doesn't jump on them. If your dog doesn't end up doing the jumping, then your friend can pull out a treat and throw it on the floor for the dog to tell them they did a good job.

You will not want to have other people coming to your home and training your dog, which is why we are doing this step now. If you do this training process in the right manner, other people can then come into your home, as loud and excited as they would like, and your dog will sit and wait until they want to pet the dog, rather than having the dog jumping on them.

Pulling on the Leash

The next thing that we need to look at when it comes to training your dog is when they try to pull on the leash. This is a big issue that a lot of dogs are going to face when they first get started, and it is one that you are able to break within a few weeks if you decide to go out on walks enough and work with some of the training techniques in this book.

If you have already gone through and done some of the foundation work for this collar and even tried training without the collar, but you still find that the dog gets excited or wants to pull against you and the leash, there are a few more methods that you are able to use to make this work.

One technique that is often used for these persistent pullers is known as the stop and pop method. With this method, you are going to take the dog out on a walk with a leash that is about six to eight feet long. You want to go with a leash that is at least this long because it gives them more room while you do the training.

At the moment, right before the dog starts pulling on this leash, you will need to stop quickly and tap on the continuous button at the exact same time. A good level with this one is to set it at 10 levels or so higher than what you know the working level to be. If you find that this is not enough and the dog insists on pulling against the leash, then you can increase the level some more until you have a dog who is walking but also leaving some slack on the leash.

This is just one of the techniques that you are able to use with your dog. Another option for pulling on the leash is the pressure/release technique. With this one, you are going to add on a low to medium level continuous pressure every time that the dog starts to pull. Then, when they stop pulling on the leash and allow for a little bit of slack, you can stop pulling. You can adjust the levels on the device based on what works for your dog.

Remember that this means that you will probably need to use the shock a bit more on the dog until they figure out what is causing it and what will make it stop for them. Some people don't like to work with this method because you end up pushing the button more. But for some dogs, this is the method that is going to work the best for getting the dog to listen to you and do what you would like.

How to Work with More Than One Dog at a Time

Another thing that you may have to encounter when it is time to work with training with this collar is if you have more than one dog at a time. When you are trying to train more than one dog with this kind of collar, it is often best if you are able to train each dog on their own, at least until each dog is doing well. When they are doing this, you can start to work on the dogs at the same time. You will need to be patient with this and remember that when you are training two or more dogs, it is going to take some time to help you get adjusted and to make sure both will behave.

While you are doing this, keep in mind that the collar is going to only deliver stimulation to one collar at a time. This means that you cannot press two or more stimulation buttons at the time because the radio frequency that comes with it is going to block both signals.

This can be a pain if both dogs are causing issues for you. If you find that both dogs are running away from you and you would like to call them both back at the same time, you have to get the attention of just one. Picking out the dog who is leading the chase and getting them to turn around can often help make this work better.

Predatory Chasing

This process is going to be simple, but as a new trainer, it is easy to make it too complicated with unnecessary and complex protocols. You need to start out by determining which animals you are fine with your dog chasing around and which animals they should not chase. It is probably best if you are able to prevent them from chasing any animal at all. This way, you can avoid any confusion, but you can really pick out which animals are fine and which ones are not.

When your dog happens to see an animal that they are not supposed to be chasing, you can say come, wait for a second, and see if they are going to come back to you. If they don't, then you can hold onto the continuous button on the collar. It is best to start this one with the normal working level, and then you can increase the level as needed if you find that the dog is not responding to you or not.

If the dog is not responding to the controller that you have, you may have to dial it up pretty quickly. More times than not, you will hear your dog vocalize a bit and then stop. Once this happens, you will be able to call the dog back, and you should not use the collar for this part. Once the dog comes back, turn down the level on the collar and continue on with the walk. Or, you can have the choice to put the dog back on the leash if it is needed at this point.

This is a process that is best done on an e collar that has the versatility to hold down the button continuously and increase the level all at the same time. It is best if you are able to continually hold down the button and then increase the level quickly until your dog stops. If the collar is not able to increase the level without releasing the button, then you need to be able to give the command, hold down the button, release the button, increase the level and then reapply.

How far should my dog be able to range away from me?

This is going to depend on what you are comfortable with, how well your dog is at listening, and the area you are in. For the times when you are in an area that is not safe and has a lot of traffic, and so on, then you will want to keep the dog closer to you. But when playing in the park or somewhere safe, and you know that your dog is good at listening, then it is fine for you to let the dog get a bit further away.

You will find that at the beginning of your training, it is best if the dog is not allowed to range too far from you. As the dog is better at training, you can choose if you would like to let the dog go further. For the most part, the dog is able to keep within fifty to one hundred feet to make the training effective. However, the best idea is to make sure that the dog never gets out of your sight at all during the training, and otherwise, so that you can watch for anything that may cause them danger.

Training your dog with the e collar is going to be something that takes you a little bit of time to do. And it may seem like you have to almost restart with all of the different behaviors. But over time, you will get used to working with the collar, and your dog will learn the drill. And before you know it, the dog is going to start behaving, and you won't even need to use the collar any longer.

Conclusion

Thank you for making it through to the end of *E Collar Training*, let's hope it was informative and able to provide you with all of the tools you need to achieve your goals, whatever they may be.

The next step is to get started with this method of training and ensure that it is the right one that you and your dog are going to stick with. There are a lot of methods of training your dog, and the e collar is not meant to replace any of them. It is meant to make sure that you are able to properly train your dog, along with some of the other methods that you may decide to use.

If the e collar is part of your training plan, then it is time to go and purchase one o these collars for your dog. You can then try it out by seeing how to get it to fit on the dog and seeing which stimulation level is going to work the best for them. This guidebook is full of the information that you need to make this happen and to ensure that you are able to get the collar to work properly for you and your dog. Once that is all set up, you will be able to go through and work on some of the training examples that we listed to get your dog to do what you want, whether you are there or not.

This guidebook spent some time talking about e collar training and all of the neat things that you can do with it. When you are ready to make training your dog easier, and to enhance some of the other training methods that you may be using, make sure to check out this guidebook and see exactly how e collar training can work for you!

Finally, if you found this book useful in any way, a review is always appreciated!

Lightning Source UK Ltd.
Milton Keynes UK
UKHW030634050121
376432UK00007B/881